BOOKKEEPING AND ADMINISTRATION FOR THE HWBI

By Elvira Bellegoni

Published by:

Etta Publishing Company

P.O. Box 32365

Cleveland, Ohio 44132 U.S.A.

First printing 1998

Printed in the United States of America

ISBN 0-9662542-0-1

Elvira Bellegoni has been a practicing accountant since 1976. All through her accounting career she has been an instructor at various colleges and universities. She has published many articles dealing with the smaller business, from preparing a Business Plan to Tax Planning, to Growth Strategies. She has extensively lectured on the same subjects. Over the last 10 years she has been a frequent volunteer lecturer for SCORE (Senior Council Of Retired Executives)

To P.R.B., *Thank you.*

BOOKKEEPING AND ADMINISTRATION

FOR THE SMALLER BUSINESS
TABLE OF CONTENTS

BOOKKEEPING AND ADMINISTRATION
FOR THE SMALLER BUSINESS
PREFACE

Bookkeeping, complete and accurate, is not a hard task to accomplish.

This book is meant to teach you how to record business transactions and how to properly organize and retain your documentation. Accounting is beyond the scope of this book. Accounting is much more comprehensive than bookkeeping although accounting does include bookkeeping.

Accounting is the means by which financial data is analyzed and reported. Bookkeeping is the recording of the financial data.

If you own a business you will need a good accountant--a proper bookkeeping system allows you to keep accurate and timely data but you will still need an accountant to analyze and report the data; however, if you do keep a proper bookkeeping system the accountant's fees will certainly be much lower than if you did not have a proper system.

The author strongly suggests that, unless you are proficient in bookkeeping, you retain the services of an accountant to determine that the entire bookkeeping system you plan to implement is the best for your company, to determine how certain financial data should be recorded, and for the preparation of financial statements. The author also suggests that financial statements be prepared on a regular basis (e.g. monthly, quarterly, etc.) and on a timely basis.

A complete and accurate bookkeeping system will:

1. facilitate the preparation of financial statements and tax returns,

2. allow you to obtain a better understanding of the financial position and operating

   results of the business, and

3. reduce professional services fees.

BOOKKEEPING AND ADMINISTRATION
FOR THE SMALLER BUSINESS
INTRODUCTION

This book has been written with the following readers in mind:

1. The entrepreneur, either already in business or about to start a venture. Many businesses are started because of an idea. The new entrepreneur knows that he or she has a good product or a good service to be provided. The skills available are usually those pertaining to the business idea, not about bookkeeping and paperwork. The entrepreneurs needs to have some idea of what is involved in running a company from a bookkeeping and administration standpoint. The information that is presented in this book provides a background in these areas.

2. The employee, who perhaps wants to better his or her skills and enter the world of business. Often, new business ventures are made up of the entrepreneur who has a good idea and family friends, all eager to help but lacking certain basic skills.

3. For re-entry into the work force individuals. Office and bookkeeping skills are fundamental and necessary skills which must exist in every company. A look at 'want ads' demonstrates a continued need for these skills; therefore, this book should be very useful to those who need to learn new skills.

4. Students, who have never learned bookkeeping in high schools, or need a refresher before taking college accounting. For students, this book covers what an introductory accounting textbook covers in many of its chapters.

BOOKKEEPING AND ADMINISTRATION
FOR THE SMALLER BUSINESS

Elvira Bellegoni, MBA, CPA

FIRST EDITION

ETTA Publishing Company

SECTION 1

WHAT AND WHEN TO RECORD

What to record

EVERYTHING that has to do with the business and which can be expressed in dollars and cents must be recorded.

It is extremely important to record everything on paper. Although most of us can claim to have a good memory, when we are busy, worried or tired it is easy to forget UNLESS we have recorded the information down on paper. At times you will encounter a transaction which you do not know how or where to record it--jot it down--what it is (in your own words) and the dollar amount involved. You can just use a notebook, call it 'The Pending Items' notebook. As these pending matters are resolved, just so note in your notebook.

When to Record

Ideally, as soon as the transaction takes place. At times this is not possible for a variety of reasons, including lack of time and or personnel. However, you should decide on when to record the transactions and stick to that decision. For example, you might decide that every Tuesday and Friday evenings you will update all your records. Remember that the longer you wait to update your records, the harder it is going to be. Trying to remember what happened a week ago and reconstructing data always takes much more time than doing a complete and accurate job when you are supposed to.

Please note that in the event of an audit from a taxing authority, if you present information that is properly and neatly recorded and organized, your chances of a more favorable outcome and expedient completion of such an audit are greatly enhanced.

SECTION 2

THE BASIC JOURNALS

There are five basic journals which businesses use in their bookkeeping systems. The particular content of each journal is tailored to the specific needs of the company; however, there is information which is common to all companies. Some companies may use additional journals for the purpose of better organizing and segregating certain business transactions. These journals will be briefly described throughout the text.

This journal contains only one item: SALES THAT WERE MADE ON CREDIT--nothing else. (That means that 'cash' sales are not recorded in this journal.) The sales journal can be structured as follows:

Date	Name	Invoice #	Terms	Sales Amount + Sales Tax = Total

Explanation of the Sales Journal:

Date- the date the credit sale was made

Name- this is the name of the customer to whom you sold the merchandise

Invoice #- This is your invoice number. Every business who sells on credit should send (or give) the customer an invoice detailing the sale. If you have a retail business you would probably give your customers a sales slip. Both the invoice and the sales slip should be numbered and issued sequentially; that is, in numerical order.

Terms- This refers to when the customer must pay and to possible discounts you give to your customers as an incentive to them to pay the invoice promptly. For example, let us say that you sold merchandise for $100 to the AXA Company. Your terms are '2/10, N/30 (reads like this: 2 10 net 30.) What these terms mean is that the AXA Company is entitled to a 2% discount if it pays within 10 days of invoice date, otherwise it has to pay the full amount (net) within 30 days of invoice date. (Note: when you see terms as the example given above, 2/10, N/30, the first number refers to the percentage of discount, the second number refers to how fast, in number of days, the customer has to pay to obtain the discount, the 'N' stands for net but it means the full purchase price, and the last number, 30, refers to the last day the customer has to pay the invoice before it becomes past due.

Continuing with the example above, if the AXA Company pays within the discount period, it will receive a $2.00 discount , and therefore, pay $98.00:

Amount of sale: $100.00

Discount: $2.00 ($100.00 times .02)

Amount to be paid: $98.00

Sales amount-This is simply the amount of the gross sale.

Sales tax-If you sell to final consumers, you will have to charge sales tax (see section 8). The sales tax you collect from your customers will have to be remitted to the proper governmental agency.

Total-This is the total amount your customer owes you. This is also called 'Account Receivable.'

Your sales journal might need to have one or more additional columns (e.g. you ship the merchandise to your customers and you charge them for the shipping costs.)

PURCHASE JOURNAL

This journal contains only one item: PURCHASE OF MERCHANDISE ON CREDIT-- nothing else. If merchandise is purchased for cash, it will not be recorded in this journal.

NOTE: If you do not sell merchandise you do not need this journal.

The Purchase Journal can be structured as follows:

| Invoice date | Name of vendor | Vendor Invoice # | Terms | Amount |

Explanation of the Purchase Journal headings:

Invoice Date- The date printed on the invoice

Name of Vendor- This is the name of the vendor from whom you purchased the merchandise

Terms- refers to when you are supposed to pay the invoice and if you are entitled to a discount for paying within a certain number of days.

Amount- This is the amount you have to pay. There are two ways to record the amount:

   (1) it can be recorded at the gross amount, or

   (2) it can be recorded at the net amount (that is, the gross amount less the discount.)

The second method is used by companies whose policy is to *always* pay within the discount period.

NOTE: If the vendor allows you a discount for paying within a period of time, do pay within the discount period and take the discount. In most instances it is advantageous to do so.

Example: We buy merchandise for a total price of $1,000.00. The terms are 1/10, N/30. If we pay in ten days we save $10.00 (1,000.00 times .01) and pay $990.00. If we do not get the discount we have another 20 days to pay, except, that we will have to pay the full $1,000.00. Therefore, we may say that we could have kept the money in the bank earnings, let say 10% per year, for an additional 20 days. How much interest would we earn if we kept the $990 in the bank for an additional 20 days?

990.00 times 10% divided by 360 days times 20 days equals $5.42!!

As you can see, if we pay within the discount period and get a 1% discount ($10.00) we are better off by $4.58 than if we had paid 20 days later! (A $10.00 discount compared with $5.42 that could have been earned in interest.)

In this journal we record the cash received--regardless of where the cash comes from. For example, cash received from customers to whom we had sold on credit, cash received from customers from cash sales, cash received from a bank loan, cash received as a refund, and so on, is all recorded in the Cash Receipts Journal. Remember-ALL the cash that is received (and that includes checks and credit card sales), is recorded in the Cash Receipts Journal.

A sample of the Cash Receipts Journal could be as follows:

Date	Name/ Description	Amount Received	Accounts Receivable	Less Discount	Cash Sale	Other Cash Received

Date- the date the cash was received

*Name/Description-*Name of payer and reason for payment (A description is really needed only for 'Other Cash Received'

*Amount Received-*The actual payment you received

The next four items, 'credit sale collected',' less discount',' cash sale' and 'other cash received' are to show where the 'amount received' came from.

*Credit Sale-*this is the gross amount the customer owed you

Less discount-this is the amount of the discount the customer has taken for paying within the discount period

Cash Sale-this represents the amount of the cash sale

Other Cash Received-this represents all other cash which was received .

There may be transactions which only partially involve cash receipts. For example, you sell $500 worth of merchandise and your customer gives you a down payment of $200 with the remainder ($300) to be paid at a later date (by the way, the $300 is now an Account Receivable!)

The above transaction gets recorded in the Cash Receipts Journal. Therefore, we can say that transactions involving any type of cash receipt gets recorded in the Cash Receipts Journal. If you are asking yourself: Can't I record $200 as a cash sale and $300 as a credit sale? the answer is YES; however, if you have more than a very few transactions like this, you would actually be complicating the recording function.

One more thing on the Cash Receipts Journal. You were told that credit card sales are recorded in this journal. The reason is that those credit card receipts are as good as cash because as soon as you deposit them the bank gives you credit the same as when you deposit cash or checks.

Some companies do prefer to have a separate journal called 'Credit Card Sales' and you may want to do so if you believe this would help you.

The Cash Payment Journal requires that you record in this journal all the cash that is paid out--regardless of what is being paid; therefore, either you are paying the rent, or repaying a loan, or giving a refund to a customer, all the cash paid out is recorded in this journal. As was the case with the Cash Receipts Journal, any transaction involving any type of cash payment gets recorded in the Cash Payment Journal. For example, if you buy office furniture for $2,000 and you give a down payment of $500, this transaction gets recorded in the Cash Payment Journal.

A sample of this journal could be as follows:

Date	*Name*	*Check #*	*Amount*	*Merchandise*	*Payroll*	*etc.*	*etc.*	*etc.*	*Other*

As you can see, this journal has a column for 'check #'. It is a good idea to always use a check for payment. At times this is not feasible, e.g. using a check to buy a postage stamp. In this case you will want to set up a 'Petty Cash' system which is described in Section 4.

How many columns the Cash Payment Journal should have or which headings to use is to be decided based upon which transactions occur frequently in your company. For example, if every week you buy merchandise and every week you pay employees, it would be more efficient to have a column called 'merchandise' and one called 'payroll' and so on. On the other hand, it probably is not very useful to have a column just for 'rent' as rent is only paid once a month. In this instance, you would have a column called 'other' under which you would record transactions which occur no more than once or twice a month.

This journal is used when a transaction cannot be recorded into any of the other journals. For example, a customer returns merchandise which he/she had purchased on credit and not paid for yet. (The information for the original sale would have already been recorded in the 'Sales Journal'.)

To determine if this transaction should be recorded in the General Journal ask yourself the following questions:

   1. Did we sell something in this transaction? No, this is a return, not a sale and therefore, the 'Sales Journal' cannot be used.

   2. Did we buy inventory? No; therefore, we cannot use the 'Purchase Journal'.

   3. Did we pay cash or write a check? No; therefore, the 'Cash Payment Journal' cannot be used.

   4. Did we receive cash or a check? No; therefore, the Cash Receipts Journal cannot be used.

Because none of the four journals can be used, the General Journal must be used.

Another example: We bought office supplies on credit. Our first thought might be to go to the Purchase Journal; however, a review of the Purchase Journal tells us that only purchases of merchandise on credit should be recorded in that journal. The other journals clearly cannot be used; therefore, we have to record this transaction in the General Journal.

In order for you to understand how the transactions can be recorded in the General Journal, you have to know the rules about journal entries. See Section 9 for a discussion of journal entries. If, after having gone through Section 9, you are still uncertain, ask your accountant to help you. He/she can tell you how to best do the recording to facilitate the preparation of the financial statements.

OTHER JOURNALS

There is another commonly used journal: the Payroll Journal.

If you have employees you will have to keep a Payroll Journal. This journal is indispensable in determining amounts owed for tax withholdings (IRS, state, city, etc.), employer's tax liability, and of course, to prepare the annual W-2s.

A Payroll Journal can be structured as follows:

Date	Name	Check #	Amount	Gross Pay	FICA	Medicare	Federal	State	City	Net Pay

Note: on the Cash Disbursement Journal you will only need to record the total amount of the net pay. You do not need other detail as the individual amounts and check numbers are already shown in the Payroll Journal.

SECTION 3

SUBSIDIARY LEDGERS

The word 'subsidiary' as used here means any accounting records which show detailed information, by customer or by vendor, of transactions that have occurred within a period of time and other valuable information.

There are two basic types of Subsidiary Ledgers, one for Accounts Receivable and one for Accounts Payable. (Some companies use additional Subsidiary Ledgers depending on their need for detailed information.)

Accounts Receivable-it shows: who owes you what, how fast/slow they pay for their credit purchases, how much business they have done with you over a period of time, etc.

Accounts payable-it shows to whom you owe money and how much, when the bills should be paid, the credit terms the vendor gives you, etc.

Let us first talk about the Accounts Receivable subsidiary ledger. Based upon the journals described so far, how can you find out who owes you money? With a lot of pain!! First you would have to look at the Sales Journal to determine how much you sold on credit to the customer. Next, you would have to go through the Cash Receipts Journal to find out how much the customer has paid. You may also have to go to the General Journal to find out if the customer had returned merchandise, and so on. Clearly, this system would be extremely inefficient and the potential for making errors is great. So, here comes the Accounts Receivable Subsidiary Ledger to the rescue. (You may now want to quickly take a look on page 43 for a sample customer card. As you can see, you can just pull out the customer's file to have a complete history as well as the current status of that account.

In order for this system to work properly, every time (NO exceptions!) a transaction occurs that involves a customer, you have to record the transaction in the proper journal and then record the same transaction in the customer's file.

Example:

On October 1 you sold merchandise on credit to the XWW Company for $1,000.
Record the sale in the Sales Journal AND in the customer's file.

The XWW Company returns $200 worth of merchandise on October 3.
Record the return in the General Journal AND in the customer's file.

On October 9 you receive a check for $800 from the XWW Company. ($1,000 less the return of $200)

Record the payment in the Cash Receipts Journal AND in the customer's file.
The Accounts Receivable subsidiary ledger can be a valuable planning tool. In addition to showing the dollar amount of business that was transacted with a customer and the payment history, you can use the same information for these purposes:

1. Has there been an increase or a decrease in the sales to this customer?

2. WHY have sales increased or decreased?

3. WHAT items has this customer bought from us during the last month, quarter, etc.?

4. HOW can we increase the current business with this customer? (E.g. offer additional products, better pricing, etc.)

5. Based upon the level of business transacted and the items bought, is there anything we can do to obtain better customer loyalty?

The same system is used for the Accounts Payable Subsidiary Ledger. For example, *you buy merchandise* on *credit*. You record it in the Purchase Journal and in the Vendor's file. When *you pay the bill* you record it in the Cash Payment Journal AND in the vendor's file.

You can also use the Accounts Payable subsidiary ledger as a planning tool. For example, you may determine that, based upon the level of business you have transacted with this vendor, and your payment history, you should be entitled to a discount or to better prices, and so on.

There are two other commonly used Subsidiary Ledgers: the Payroll and the Fixed Assets.

The Payroll Subsidiary Ledger consists of having one file (card) per employee showing all information as it appears in the Payroll Journal. This ledger will also contain the employee's address, social security number, marital status, exemptions claimed, title, pay rate, and other pertinent information. Tax filing requirements require that you report wages and withholding information per employee on a quarterly and annual basis. For example, some states require that on a quarterly basis you report the gross wages and hours worked per employee to the Bureau of Employment Services. Some states also require that you report the gross pay and state tax withheld per employee on a quarterly basis. Every year you also have to furnish to the Social Security Administration and (where required) states and municipalities W-2s for each employee.

The Fixed Assets Subsidiary Ledger will show information about specific assets which have been capitalized and are being depreciated. This individual up-to-date information is needed when filing business income tax returns and in the event of an insurance claim.

The typical Fixed Assets subsidiary ledger will show the following information (per type of asset):

1. Date of purchase

2. Vendor name and location

3. Cost of the asset

4. Date paid

5. How paid (e.g. check#___)

6. Description of the asset purchased, and

7. Location of the assets (e.g. which office if you have more than one office.)

Additional information may be the method of depreciation used, the amount of depreciation to be taken every period, and for how long (usually expressed in years) the asset will be depreciated.

It also is a good idea to do the following:

1. On the back of the subsidiary ledger have a copy of the vendor's invoice and

2. A picture of the asset purchased.

PETTY CASH

If you recall, when discussing the Cash Payment Journal, it was mentioned that when it is not feasible to pay everything with a check, you should use 'Petty Cash'.

Here is how it works:

Write a check for $100 or $200 (you have to decide how much cash you will need in one month for minor expenditures) made payable to the person who will be in charge of the Petty Cash funds. (By the way, where do you record the check you are writing? In the Cash Payment Journal, of course!) When the check is cashed the person in charge of it will put it in a LOCKED BOX. This cash will then be used for small-amount purchases. You are not to use Petty Cash to cash employees checks, make small loans, and so forth. Remember why you are establishing a Petty Cash system and use it for its intended purpose only.

Every time this cash is used, a slip of paper, called 'voucher' (available at every office supply store--as are journals and ledgers) is to be filled out listing what was purchased and the amount of the purchase. In addition, the receipt (you should always get a receipt for whatever you spend) should be stapled to the voucher. At the end of the month summarize how much Petty Cash was spent and replenish it (write a check) for exactly the amount which was spent.) This means that every month, on the first of the month, you will have the same amount of petty cash you started with.

Example: on October 1 you establish a Petty Cash system. You write a check for $100 payable to Ms. Belles who will be in charge of the petty cash funds. During October you spent the following amounts:

Postage............................$11.20

Office supplies...................32.35

Delivery charges...............13.52

Total spent..........................$57.07

On October 30 you would write a check for $57.07 payable to Ms. Belles, to replenish the petty cash funds; therefore, you start the new month, November, again with $100.00.

SECTION 5

BANK RECONCILIATION

Bank reconciliations should be prepared every month for every bank account a company has. In addition, bank reconciliations should be done as soon as possible after receiving the bank statements.

Preparing bank reconciliations will:

1. Allow you to determine the true cash balances

2. Allow you to properly update your accounting records

3. Allow you to have a better grasp of your cash situation.

4. To promptly correct errors. Financial institutions (actually, the people who work on your account) do make mistakes too. Do not assume that financial institutions do not make mistakes.

You might have noticed on occasion that what the bank statement shows as the cash balance at the end of a particular month is different than what your checkbook balance shows on that day. The reasons for the discrepancies are as follows:

1. The bank has taken cash out of your account (or added to it) during a month, but you did not know about it, and

2. The bank was not aware of certain transactions that took place during the month and which you have properly recorded in your checkbook (and in the accounting records.)

Examples:

  1. You made a deposit at the end of the month. You properly recorded the cash/checks you received in your accounting records and in your checkbook; however, the bank received the deposit too late to be recorded that day. The bank will record that deposit the next day (which is NEXT month.) In this instance, the bank was not aware of a cash transaction that took place that day, but you were. You recorded the cash/checks received, the bank did not. So, in the bank statement, where 'deposits' are listed, that one deposit will not appear.

  2. Checks #105, #110, and #111 which you wrote during the month, and you properly deducted those amounts from your checkbook and also recorded them in your Cash Payments Journal, were not returned by the bank. The bank was not aware of these payments and therefore, did not deduct those amounts from your account. Those checks will clear (be paid by the bank) in the next month. This is another transaction where you updated your checkbook but the bank did not.

  3. There are some items however, which the bank recorded (that is, increases and/or decreases in your cash balance) but you did not because you did not know about them. Examples of there transactions are bank service charges, check printing charges, bad checks ('non-sufficient funds' checks), etc.

The bank reconciliation is done in two parts. First you start with the 'Balance per Bank' and add to and/or deduct from items which are found in your checkbook but do not appear in the bank statement. This items usually are 'deposits in transit' and 'outstanding checks'.) You now have an 'Adjusted Balance per Bank'.

Next, you start with the 'Balance per Checkbook' and add to/deduct from it items which appear in the bank statement but not in your checkbook. (The most common example is service charges.) You now have an 'Adjusted Balance per Checkbook'. If the reconciliation is done correctly, the 'Adjusted Balance per Bank' amount should be the same as the 'Adjusted Balance per Checkbook.'

After the bank reconciliation has been completed, there remains one task to perform; that is, to update your checkbook and the accounting records for all items that appear under the 'Balance per Checkbook'. The journal you use to record these items is the General Journal. Although cash is involved in most if not all of these transactions, it would be too cumbersome to go to the Cash Receipts Journal, the Cash Payment Journal, and the General Journal.

SECTION 6

PAYROLL TAXES

Every business who has employees is responsible for filing payroll tax returns and paying payroll taxes.

The following taxes are to be withheld from the employees paychecks:

1. Social Security and Medicare
2. Federal Income Tax
3. State Income Tax
4. Local income tax.

It is your responsibility to withhold these taxes and remit them to the proper governmental agencies (along with the payroll tax returns.)

The Internal Revenue Service has a publication, 'Circular E' which contains and explains all the rules and regulations concerning payroll taxes, including how much to withhold, when to pay the taxes, how to make those payments, and when to file tax returns. You may obtain one copy (free of charge) by calling your nearest IRS office.

Not all States and localities require withholding of income taxes; however, most due. In Ohio, for example, it is mandatory to withhold income taxes and the State has a publication similar to the IRS 'Circular E'.

Local taxes, when required to be withheld, are usually a fixed percentage of gross pay.

Besides the taxes to be withheld from the employees' paychecks, there are some taxes which are levied on the employer, for example, the employer must match the social security and Medicare taxes withheld and pay federal unemployment (these items are also covered in the 'Circular E'). The employer must also pay state unemployment and workers' compensation.

If you are self employed, either you have employees or not, you have to pay social security and Medicare taxes (called Self Employed tax.) The tax rate is multiplied by the *net profits* of the business and not on the money you take out of the business. Self employed individuals are not deemed to be employees of the company and, therefore, do not get a wage or a salary. The money taken out is called a 'withdrawal'. Because there is not a payroll for the self employed individual, the Internal Revenue Service requires every self employed individual to pay social security and Medicare taxes based upon the net profits of the business. If instead or a profit there is a loss, or the profit is less than $400 there is no social security or Medicare taxes.

There are rather severe consequences (in terms of interest and penalties) for not filing or filing late and for paying late. It is suggested that you do the following two things:

1. Call the IRS, state and local income tax departments, the Bureau of Employment Services and the Bureau of Workers' Compensation. Tell them you have/will have employees and you need to know what to do. They will send you all the information and forms you need.

2. Open a savings account and use this account to deposit all the payroll taxes withheld from the employees plus the taxes the employer must pay (your accountant will explain to you how to determine how much to deposit) so that when it is time to pay these taxes, the funds will be available. You must disciple yourself to deposit this money every time you pay the employees and use this money ONLY to pay payroll taxes. You must think of this 'tax'

money as not being yours. In fact, it is not yours, it belongs to the various taxing authorities.

One word of caution: if your business is a corporation, everyone that works for the corporation is an employee, and that includes you even if you are the sole owner. It also includes any member of your family that works for the company and gets paid.

SECTION 7
OTHER TAXES

In addition to payroll taxes (and of course income taxes) you may be liable for filing and paying other taxes, for example, sales tax and taxable business property tax.

SALES TAX

If you sell merchandise to the final consumer, or provide certain services, you must charge sales tax. You also would need to have a vendor's license. Because what is a taxable sale or service varies from state to state and from county to county, call the county in which your business is located to determine if you are subject to a vendor's license and sales tax collection.

TAXABLE BUSINESS PROPERTY

Some states require that a return be filed and taxes be paid on assets (e.g. merchandise held for sale, equipment used, etc.). This is usually administered at the county level.

OTHER TAXES

Because there are different requirements from state to state, you are urged to contact your state to determine if you are liable for any other returns/payments of taxes.

Most states have compiled booklets that briefly describe and explain all the tax filing and paying requirements for businesses. These booklets are available for any business requesting them.

SECTION 8

INTERNAL DOCUMENTATION AND FILINGS SYSTEM

All documentation generated by your business needs to be retained and filed properly. Do not discard any voided (not used) documentation. The voided documents should be kept to account for the sequence of the documents used, and would aid in the reconstruction of business transactions. Your should have a folder labeled 'Voided Documents' in which you keep all voided documents.

Common internal documentation found in any company is:

  1. Sales Receipts

  2. Sales Invoices

  3. Monthly statements

  4. Purchase orders

  5. Checks

  6. Memos.

Sales Receipts: **It is a good and necessary practice to always have a written record of all cash sales made. It is practically impossible to keep track of the sales made and the cash received during the day unless you have the sales receipts. The type of business you have will dictate the exact content of the sales receipt. The sales receipts should be numbered and issued sequentially. The sales receipt must be at least in duplicate: the original goes to the customer and the second copy should be filed in a folder marked 'Sales Receipts--Cash Sales.' (Most cash registers have duplicate tapes inside the register. One copy is given to the customer and the other remains in the register until it is time to put in a new roll.)**

Store all of your documentation in a safe place. By law, you are required to keep certain documentation for a period of one year, three years, seven years, or permanently.

At the library you will be able to find books that show the 'record retention period' for documents. Appendix A illustrates the Record Retention Period for various documentation.

Sales Invoice: The sales invoice is usually used for credit sales. The invoice should be in triplicate. The original is sent to the customer, one copy is filed under 'Revenue' or 'Income' or 'Sales' and the last copy is filed in the accounts receivable folder. The invoices should be numbered and issued sequentially (so that you can account for all sales made.) If there is documentation pertaining to that invoice, for example the customer's purchase order and/or shipping documents, they should all be stapled to the invoice filed under 'Revenue.'

With regard to the sales invoice, when a customer pays an invoice:

1. Take that invoice out of the 'accounts receivable' folder, stamp (or write on it) 'PAID', the date the payment was received, and the amount received. (Do not forget your journals and ledgers--Cash Receipts Journal and Accounts Receivable Subsidiary Ledger.)

2. This 'paid' sales invoice will then be filed in a folder appropriately called 'Paid Sales Invoices'.

If a customer sends only a partial payment do step 1. above; however, leave the invoice in the 'Accounts Receivable' folder until that invoice is paid in full and then proceed with step #2 above.

Monthly Statements: It is good business practice to send monthly statements to all customers who owe you money as a reminder to them that they have a liability to you. The exact format of this statement depends on your particular needs.

Sending statements to customers fulfills these objectives:

1. To remind them to pay, as stated above

2. To provide your company with an added control feature by:

a. correcting errors as soon as possible. For example, if the customer's records show he/she already paid, it is very likely that he/she would let you know right-away. You would then proceed to determine the reason for the discrepancy,

b. acting as a deterrent to employee fraud.

Purchase Orders: Some companies use 'Purchase Orders' whenever purchasing items, (perhaps items costing more than a certain amount). Two major advantages of a purchase order are:

1. To know exactly what was ordered and what the cost is, and

2. To control purchases. For example, no purchase can be made and/or paid for unless it was properly approved with a purchase order.

Purchase orders should be in duplicate or triplicate, should be numbered, and should be issued sequentially. (Original to the vendor, one copy to the receiving department, and one copy in the 'pending orders' file.

When the vendor's invoice has been received, the invoice should be compared to the receiving report, if any, and with the purchase order. If there are no discrepancies, all documentation should be stapled together.

Checks: All checks should be prenumbered and issued sequentially. As was discussed before, no internal documentation should be destroyed or discarded. If you void a check, write across it (front and back) 'VOID'. If the check had already been signed, tear off the signature portion. File the voided check in the 'Voided Documents' folder.

A word of caution with checks: NEVER write checks made payable to the order of 'cash'. If such a check is lost, anyone who finds it can cash it and you have no recourse because the work 'cash' means pay the check to whomever is presenting it to be cashed.

Credit Memos: These memos are sent to customers when you are decreasing the amount which the customer owes you. An example of a transaction using a credit memo is as follows: The ABC Company returns $200 worth of merchandise because it was sent in error or it was damaged. You now have the merchandise back and the customer does not owe you the $200 anymore. (Of course, you would record this transaction in the General Journal and then in the Accounts Receivable Subsidiary Ledger, right?) You would fill out a Credit Memo and send it to the customer. You should retain a copy of the Credit Memo, which means that it should be in duplicate.

Any other documentation: Thus far we have mostly discussed 'internally generated' documentation. Any documentation (internally or externally) generated needs to be retained and filed properly.

Get organized. Obtain a good supply of folders, labels, and filing cabinets. The most organized your documentation is the easier it will be to use that information to:

1. Back up your financial statements,

2. to prepare tax returns,

3. to reply to queries from vendors, customers, etc., and

4. to plan.

It is strongly suggested that you take a 'walk -through' an office supplies store to familiarize yourself with the forms and documents available. You will be able to find just about all forms, documents, journals, ledgers, memos, etc. that we have discussed in this book.

MANUALS

Any company, regardless of its size, should develop company manuals. There are three very common manuals:

1. Operating Procedures Manual

2. Personnel Manual

3. Accounting/bookkeeping Manual

1. Operating Procedures Manual

This manual describes your business in terms of the various tasks and operations to be performed and all the forms that need to be used to documents the tasks and procedures performed. It really is a detailed description of:

1. What needs to be done

2. Who is going to do it

3. How it is going to be done

4. When it is going to be done, and

5. What documentation is needed throughout the process.

Lines or communication (who reports to whom), authority, and responsibility are also specified.

2. Personnel Manual

This manual contains all the policies of the company regarding personnel. The most common items contained in a Personnel Manual are:

1. Hours of operations, overtime pay, vacation pay, paid absences, payroll period.

2. Causes for dismissal.

3. Benefits provided by the company

4. Promotions

5. Etc.

3. Accounting/bookkeeping manual.

This manual will contain a general description of business operations, forms and documents found within the company. There will be a very concise and detailed (step-by-step) description of when, how, where to make journal entries, how to do posting, and anything else the bookkeeping/accounting department is to do before the outside accountant takes over.

Documentation also includes general correspondence, notes taken during phone conversations or meetings, and inter-company memoranda. Also, and even more important, financial statements prepared by you or your accountant, any journals and ledgers, employee folders, and tax returns. (NOTE: do not throw away/destroy anything unless you are absolutely sure you can do so.)

There are three main reasons to retain any documentation:

1. Legal evidence (e.g. in the event of a lawsuit)

2. Tax evidence (e.g. in the event of an audit)

3. Planning for your business (e.g. to develop plans and budgets.)

SECTION 9

JOURNAL ENTRIES

The General Journal, as was discussed previously requires that formal accounting entries be made. These entries are based upon 'debits' and 'credits'. To understand journal entries you would need to have studied some accounting. Any Introductory Accounting textbook has detailed explanations on how to make journal entries, a few chapters are devoted exclusively to this purpose. Because of the complexity and length of such a topic, Journal Entries cannot be explained here. We do suggest that you get an Introductory Accounting book, read through the chapters that pertain to Journal Entries, and ask your accountant for assistance.

However, here is a very brief, concise explanation:

1. The General Journal is made up of two columns: the column to the left is called the 'Debit' column, and the column at the right is called the 'Credit' Column.

2. The word 'Debit' has nothing to do with owing something to somebody, and the word 'Credit' has nothing to do with credit.

3. 'Debit' stands for left, 'Credit' stands for right.

4. Certain items that make up financial statements usually have a 'Debit' (left) balance and some have a 'Credit' (right) balance.

5. Assets and expenses have a 'Debit Balance'. Liabilities, capital, and revenue have a 'Credit' balance.

6. Therefore, to increase assets or expenses you would have to debit them, to decrease them you would credit them.

7. Therefore, to increase liabilities, capital, or revenues you would have to credit them, to decrease them you would have to debit them.

8. Assets are resources the business owns, e.g. cash, accounts receivable, etc.

9. Liabilities are amounts owed to vendors and other creditors.

10. Capital is the amount owed to the owners of the business.

11. Revenue is the amount of sales or services generated by the company.

12. Expenses are costs incurred by the company to generate the revenue and other costs incurred to carry on the business.

13. All 'accounts', assets, liabilities, capital, revenue, and expenses are identified by specific name and by number, e.g. the account *CASH*, which is as asset account may be account #110, the account *ACCOUNTS RECEIVABLE*, another asset account may be account #120, etc.

14. The usual numbering sequence for accounts is: Assets 100 to 199, Liabilities 200 to 299, Capital 300 to 399, Revenue 400 to 499, and Expenses 500 to 599. (This is called a 'chart of accounts'.)

SECTION 10

INTERNAL CONTROL

Internal controls are controls a company establishes for the following reasons:

1. To ascertain that all transactions that have occurred have been properly recorded in the accounting system

2. To ascertain that all recorded transactions have in fact occurred

3. To ascertain that all transactions have been properly authorized and executed

4. To ascertain that the actual assets a company has have been compared and reconciled to what the accounting records show

5. To ascertain that its assets are properly safeguarded.

In other words Internal Controls allow a company to carry on its business in the best possible way by trying to prevent errors (intentional or non-intentional), by safeguarding its assets, and by ascertaining that the assets a company shows it has (in its accounting records) are in fact what the company physically has.

One of the important aspects of Internal Control is the *Separation of Duties*. What this means is that no employee should be allowed to carry on a transaction from beginning to end; that is, be in a position to perpetrate fraud.

The smaller the company is the harder it is to achieve good internal controls because of a lack of personnel; however, there are some basic internal control procedures that any company can take:

1. The owner should be actively involved in the business

2. Bank accounts should be reconciled on a monthly basis

3. Checks received through the mail and cash, checks, and credit card receipts obtained through over the counter sales should be deposited on a daily basis

4. Cash received from cash sales should be deposited intact; that is, none of this money should be used to pay for minor expenditures, etc.

5. No employee who works with the accounting records should also have custody of assets

6. Periodically an independent person (independent of the accounting records and of the custody of the assets) should inventory the assets. You then can compare the findings with your accounting records.

SECTION 11

SAMPLE BOOKKEEPING SYSTEM

The name of the company is Computer Consulting Company . The name of the owner is Mary Lan.

The following journals will be used (in alphabetical order):

1. Cash Payment Journal

2. Cash Receipts Journal

3. General Journal *(Records transactions not captured in the other journals)*

4. Payroll Journal

5. Services Provided Journal *(Sales Journal)*

6. Payroll Journal

Also used are (In alphabetical order):

1. Accounts Receivable Subsidiary Ledger

2. Bank reconciliation

3. Credit memo

4. Petty Cash

Transactions:

1. March 10-The company provided services to the XXZ Company and charged it $2,000 which will be paid in two weeks. Invoice #229 was used.

2. On March 11 the company issued a credit memo to XXZ Company for $100 because an error in billing was made.

3. March 12—The company also provided services to the AXA Company and charged it $3,500. $1,000 was paid immediately, and the remainder, $2,500 will be paid in two weeks.

Invoice #230 was used.

4. March 12—The company buys for cash postage stamps for 65 cents and office supplies for $12.50. The money comes out of Petty Cash which has a beginning balance of $50.

5. March 12— The company pays the following amounts with checks:

  1. Rent to Landy Company, check #121 for $1,000

  2. Office supplies from the Barron Company, check #122 for $210

6. March 27—Both the AXA Company and the XXZ Company pay for the services provided

7. March 30—The company writes the following checks:

  1. Jean Jon paycheck: Gross $1,000. The withholdings are: Social Security $62.00 and Medicare $14.50, federal income tax $150, state income tax $20, and local tax $15. The net pay is $738.50. Check #123.

  2. Petty Cash is replenished by writing check #124 made payable to Mary Lan for $13.15.

  3. Advertising costs are paid to the Whiz Company with check #125 for $125.

8. Depreciation is recorded for $200.00.

CASH RECEIPTS JOURNAL

MONTH ENDED   3/31/1999

Date	Name	Description	Amount	Cash Service	Accounts Receivable	Other
3/12	AXA Co.	see #230	1,000.00	1,000.00		
3/27	AXA Co.		2,500.00		2,500.00	
3/27	XXZ Co.		1,900.00		1,900.00	
	TOTAL		5,400.00	1,000.00	4,400.00	

CASH PAYMENTS JOURNAL

MONTH ENDED   3/31/1999

Date	Name	Check #	Amount	Supplies	Payroll	Other
3/12	Landy Co.	121	1,000.00			1,000.00 rent #530
3/12	Barron Co.	122	210.00	210.00		
3/30	Jean Jon	P.J.	738.50		738.50	
3/30	Mary Lan	124	13.15	12.50		.65 postage #590
3/30	Whiz Co.	125	125.00			125.00 advert. #540
	TOTALS		2,086.65	222.50	738.50	

① Purchase Journal

40

PAYROLL JOURNAL

MONTH ENDED   3/31/1999

Date	Name	Ck. #	Amt.	Gross	S.S.	Med.	Feder.	State	City	
3/30	Jean Jon	123	738.50	1,000.00	62.00	14.50	150.00	20.00	15.00	
	TOTALS		738.50	1,000.00	62.00	14.50	150.00	20.00	15.00	

41

SALES JOURNAL -

SERVICES PROVIDED JOURNAL

MONTH ENDED   3/31/1999

Date	Name	Invoice #	Amount	Notations
3/10	XXZ Co.	229	2,000.00	
3/12	AXA Co.	230	2,500.00	See invoice for total
	TOTALS		4,500.00	

42

ACCOUNTS RECEIVABLE SUBSIDIARY LEDGER

XXZ Company   123 Anytown Street, Colland, VS 12123

Contact: Mr. Bruno Brown

Phone: (211) 555-3333 Fax: (211) 555-2221

Client since: 1990

Rating: A

Date	Description	Debits	Credits	Balance
2/28/99	**Balance forward**			-0-
3/10	#229	2,000.00		2,000.00
3/11	① C.M. #12		100.00	1,900.00
3/27	**paid in full**		1,900.00	-0-

① CM- credit memo

ACCOUNTS RECEIVABLE SUBSIDIARY LEDGER

AXA Company P.O. Box 33, Tosall, VS 12122

Contact: Ms. Joyce Allsy

Phone: (211) 555-1661 Fax: (211) 555-6116

Client since: 1999

Rating: B+

Date	Description	Debits	Credits	Balance
3/12	#230 (1)	2,500.00		2,500.00
3/27	paid in full		2,500.00	-0-
Note: total is $3,500--	$1,000.00 paid in cash (new client)			

GENERAL JOURNAL

Date	Description	Ref. #	Debit	Credit
	Month Ended 3/31/99			
3/11	Services provided adjustments	410	100.00	
	Accounts receivable	110		100.00
	(Adjust for error made in billing)			
3/30	Depreciation Expense	575	200.00	
	Accumulated Depreciation	160		200.00
	(Record quarterly depreciation)			
3/30	Bank Charges	550	6.00	
	Cash	100		6.00
	(Record March service charges)			

BANK RECONCILIATION

	Notes	Amount
Bank reconciliation, month ended		**3/31/99**
Balance per bank		5,250.00
Plus deposits in transit		-0-
Less outstanding checks		125.00
Other		-0-
Adjusted balance per bank		5,125.00
Balance per checkbook		5,131.00
Less service charges		6.00
Less Check printing		-0-
Other		-0-
Other		-0-
Adjusted balance per checkbook		5,125.00
Outstanding Checks:		
#125	$125.00	

PETTY CASH

		Month ended 3/31/99
Beginning Balance		$50.00
Spent:		
Supplies	12.50	
Postage	.65	
Deliveries		
Other_____		
Other_____		
TOTAL SPENT		13.15
Ending Balance		36.85

Petty cash was replenished on   3/30/99 with

check #   124   for $ 13.15

COMPUTER CONSULTING COMPANY

P.O. Box 21234

Townbest, Lm 32331

CREDIT MEMO #12

To: XXZ Company

P.O. Box 32

Cleclid, Ho 12344

March 11, 1999

As pcr our phone conversation of today, this Credit Memo is to acknowledge that your account has been credited for $100.00.

Thank your for your business and your cooperation.

Sincerely,

Mary Lan,

Owner

Computer Consulting Company

Balance Sheet

March 31, 1999

ASSETS

Current Assets:

Cash, checking	5,125.00
Petty Cash	50.00
Prepaid Insurance	450.00
Total Current Assets	5,625.00

Fixed Assets:

Office Equipment	5,200.00	
Less Accumulated Depreciation	(750.00)	
Total Net Fixed Assets		4,450.00
		———
TOTAL ASSETS		10,075.00
		=======

① Current Ratio

$$\frac{\text{Current assets}}{\text{Current liabilities}} = \frac{5625}{351}$$

Shows whether your company is solvent

② Debt/Equity Ratio

$$\frac{\text{Total Debts}}{\text{Total Equity}} = \frac{351}{9724}$$

Ratio shows your ability to take on more debt.

LIABILITIES AND CAPITAL

Current Liabilities:

Taxes Payable	351.20
	———
Total Liabilities	351.20

Capital:

Mary Lan, Capital	9,723.80
	———
TOTAL LIABILITIES AND CAPITAL	10,075.00
	=======

✳ You can round up to the next whole dollar

Computer Consulting Company

Statement of Income

For the month ended March 31, 1999

Revenue:

Service Provided, net	5,400.00
	————
Total Revenue	5,400.00

Expenses:

Payroll	1,000.00
Payroll Taxes	89.10
Rent	1,000.00
Supplies	222.50
Postage	.65
Advertising	125.00
Depreciation	200.00
Bank Charges	6.00
	————
Total Expenses	2,643.25
	————
Net Profit	2,756.75
	=======

* you can round up to the next whole dollar

SECTION 12
CASH VERSUS ACCRUAL

There are two methods used to report financial information; that is, to prepare financial statements: the cash method and the accrual method. Which method is best for you depends on the type of business you have. Again, your accountant is the most qualified person to determine which method is most beneficial to you. It is important for you to know what these two methods mean, so that you will be better able to understand your financial statements.

Cash Method.

The cash method means that you are going to report revenue only when cash is received. The same holds true for expenses; that is, you report expenses only when they are paid for. There are some exceptions for expenses, the most notable has to do with merchandise. When you buy merchandise for resale you record it as an asset. When the merchandise is sold you would record a decrease in assets (you no longer have the merchandise) and you record an increase in expenses (the expense would be called Cost of Merchandise Sold.)

To give an example of how the cash method works, assume that you sell $100 worth of merchandise to a customer on credit. The customer will pay you in two weeks. When the sale takes place you do not record the sale in your accounting records. When the customer pays, then you would record the sale.

Suppose in March you get a bill from the newspaper for advertising that was done in March. You pay the bill in April. Under the cash method of accounting, you record the expense, advertising expense, only when you pay the bill, in April.

Accrual Method.

Under the accrual method transactions are recorded (reported) as they are incurred. In the example given above of the sale made to the customer who pays in two weeks, the sale would be recorded when it was made, not when the payment was received. Therefore, this transaction would give rise to a sale and an account receivable. When the customer pays, cash is increased and the account receivable is decreased.

For the advertising bill received in March, the expense would be recorded in March, not in April. Therefore, this transaction would give rise to an expense and an account payable. In April, when the advertising bill is paid, the account payable as well as cash would be decreased.

From a business standpoint which system is generally considered better? The accrual method is clearly the preferred method. It more fully shows all transactions that have taken place, regardless of when cash is received or paid out.

SECTION 13

MODIFYING THE BOOKKEEPING SYSTEM FOR GROWTH

As your business grows your bookkeeping system will have to follow suit. You will find that, as the business grows, more information needs to be assembled, needs to be broken down into finer parts, and more paperwork has to be organized. All throughout this book we talked about the fact that some companies will have additional journals and compile information to better suit their individual situations. This will be the case with your company. You will need a better system to account for your payroll and employees, both from an administrative as well as tax standpoint. You will need a better system to keep track of all your assets, and so on. As you hire more employees, your controls will need to be revised and refined. Your accountant will be the most qualified individual to help you by ascertaining your changing needs and by offering suggestions on how to modify the existing system.

One item which will make accounting for acquisitions (merchandise and anything else) simpler and more organized is what is called the '*Voucher System*'. This system replaces the *Purchase Journal* and part of the *General Journal*.

Here is how the Voucher System works:

  1. You will have to use a preprinted form called 'Voucher'. (You can develop one or buy them at an office supply store.)

  2. Anytime a bill/invoice/payroll/etc. needs to be paid a 'voucher' is filled out listing all pertinent information about that bill. As soon as the voucher is prepared it is entered in the 'Voucher Register' . The voucher Register is a journal where everything that needs to be paid in recorded; therefore, the 'purchase journal' and part of the 'general journal' is no longer needed. The bill that needs to be paid is stapled to the voucher.

3. On the face of the voucher there will be room to write the account name or number to which the bill applies. Someone in the company will have to approve the propriety of that account name or number.

4. Before a bill is paid it has to be approved for payment. Some one in the company with such authority will initial and date the voucher as approval.

5. An additional 'good point' about the 'voucher' is that the voucher requests someone in the company to check the mathematical accuracy of the bill received and some other items. This needs to be done before someone approves the bill for payment.

As you can see, the voucher system not only simplifies the bookkeeping task but also allows better internal controls to be in place.

When a company has a Voucher System the *Cash Disbursement Journal* will now be called the *Check Register*. The check register will be similar to the cash disbursement journal but much simpler.

SECTION 14

COMPUTERS AND BOOKKEEPING

We have spent a great deal of time talking about a manual bookkeeping system. If you are asking yourself why we did not talk about computers right-away because 'everybody' has one, the answer is very simple: unless you understand and 'feel' how bookkeeping works, a computer will really not help you very much. There is a saying in the computer world: 'Garbage In Garbage Out.' What this means is that if incorrect information/data is put into the computer, incorrect information/data will be the output. Another way to look at this is that without a working knowledge of how bookkeeping works and what it does, there is no way for you to determine that the computer output is correct.

Having said that, a computer will allow you to perform your bookkeeping functions in a more efficient and organized manner. You will also be able to get more and better reports.

For bookkeeping, there are many software programs that are simple and very 'user friendly'. Their cost is rather minimal. Again, a trip to your local office supply store is suggested.

Most computers in the market today come with some programs already installed. These programs usually consist of word processing programs , data base programs, charts and graphs programs, etc. Some of these programs allow you to generate your own forms; therefore, you would not have to use generic forms from an office supply store, or have a printer print them.

Your accountant (and even the computer stores) will be able to help you purchase the best hardware (computer) and software (programs) which will meet your needs.

SECTION 15
SUGGESTIONS

1. Call or visit the Internal Revenue Service, your State, your County, and your City. Ask for all information you need to start a business and to have employees. You will be amazed by how much 'free of charge' information you will get.

2. Visit your local office of the Small Business Administration and talk to a SCORE (Senior Council of Retired Executives) volunteer. Here too you will get much information and advise too!

3. Both the Internal Revenue Service and the Small Business Administration offer seminars and workshops on starting a business. Some are free of charge.

4. Many colleges and universities, in addition to regular classes, offer seminars and workshops on the same subjects.

5. We wish you *Good Luck* with your endeavors.

SECTION 16

GLOSSARY OF TERMS

Accounting

The process of analyzing and evaluating business (financial) data. It is also the process to determine how financial data should be recorded and the results presented.

Account Name

Relates to the 'chart of accounts' and it is used to identify specific accounts.

Account number

Refer to 'account name' above. Every account has its name and number too to further ascertain that the proper account is being used.

Accounts Payable

Represents moneys owed to a third party (e.g. a supplier.)

Accounts Receivable

Represents money owed to the company by a customer.

Administration

Pertains to all rules and regulations and procedures found in a company to carry on its day-to-day business activities. It relates also to documentation in terms of how to generate it, how to file it, how to store it, etc.

Assets

Assets are resources the company owns to carry on its business. Examples are, cash, accounts receivable, inventory, etc.

Bookkeeping

Bookkeeping is the process of recording data in the various journals and ledgers.

Business Transactions

Any economic event, expressed in dollar amounts, that pertains to the business of the company.

Capital

The amount the company owes to its owners. Put another way, it represents how much the owners have at stake in the company.

Credit

It applies to journal entries to represent the 'right' side of an entry.

Credit

To give credit means the company allows its customers to pay at a later date for their purchases. To obtain credit means your company is allowed to pay at a later date for its purchases.

Credit Memo

It is a letter sent to a customer reducing the balance he/she owes the company.

Debit

It applies to journal entries to refer to the 'left' side of an entry.

Depreciation

A bookkeeping entry. It is an estimate of the decrease in value, through the months or years, of an assets deemed to be fixed (of a duration of more than one year).

Deposits in Transit

Deposit made and recorded by the company but which did not clear the bank as of the end of a month.

Expenses

Expenses are the costs incurred by a company to carry on its business. Most expenses are tax deductible.

Financial Statements

All the business transactions which were recorded in the journals and the ledgers are summarized into financial statements. The two most basic financial statements are the Balance Sheet and the Statement of Income. The Balance Sheet shows, as of a certain date, all the assets, liabilities, and capital. The Statement of Income shows, for a period of time (one month, one year, etc.) all the revenues, expenses, and net profits of the business.

Fixed Assets

These assets are called fixed (sometimes they are also called long-term) because they last for a relatively long period of time. When they are purchased they become assets and through depreciation they become expenses.

Internal Controls

Any controls the company develops and implements to protect its assets as well as its accounting records.

Inventory

Also called 'merchandise' or 'merchandise inventory'. It represents all the goods the company has purchased to sell to its customers.

Journals

Journals are called 'original books of entry' because the first step in recording business transactions is done in the journals.

Ledgers

Ledgers and subsidiary ledgers summarize the transactions entered into the journals.

Liabilities

Accounts Payable are a type of liability. Liabilities is a general term representing the debts of the company.

Net Profits

The 'Bottom Figure'. It is found in the Statement of Income and it represents the difference between Revenues and Expenses.

Outstanding Checks

These are checks that were paid, recorded in the accounting records, and deducted from the checkbook but they did not clear the bank by the end of a month.

Petty Cash

It is also called 'imprest system'. It is the making available of a minor amount of moneys to pay for items when it is not possible or feasible to use checks.

Purchases

The buying of something e.g. merchandise.

Purchase Discount

A company is given a discount for paying a credit purchase within a specific number of days.

Purchase on Credit

The company is allowed to purchase items and pay for them at a later date.

Record Retention Period

By law, it is the period of time a company must retain documentation before it can dispose of it.

Revenues

Revenue (also called 'income') is a general term to represent the sales a company has made, or how much it has billed clients for services provided, etc.

Sales

The selling of merchandise to customers.

Sales Discounts

A company (the seller) allows its customers to take a discount for paying their credit purchase within a specific number of days.

Sales on Credit

The company allows its customers to buy merchandise and pay at a later date.

Separation of Duties

One of the most important parts of Internal Control. Separation of duties means that an employee that handles the accounting records should not be allowed to also have custody of assets.

Services Provided

A type of revenue generated by service companies.

Subsidiary Ledgers

Any book which details and summarizes transactions for a specific item (e.g. a customer.)

Terms

Refers to credit terms a company has with its customers and/or its vendors.

Vendor

Usually a seller of merchandise. If you sell a product, you are a vendor to your customers. If you buy products, you buy them from a vendor.

Voucher Register

A journal which lists all bills received that need to be paid.

Voucher System

A system whereby any bills that are received are recorded in a form called 'voucher'. The 'voucher' contains most of the information that is found in the bill and the voucher must be approved for payment before it can be paid.

APPENDIX A

RECORD RETENTION SCHEDULE

ONE YEAR

Bank reconciliations, routine correspondence, duplicate deposit slips, purchase orders, (except purchasing department copy), receiving sheets, requisitions, stenographer's notebooks, stockroom withdrawal forms.

THREE YEARS

General correspondence, employee personnel records (after termination), employment applications, expired insurance policies, internal audit reports, miscellaneous internal reports, petty cash vouchers, physical inventory tags, savings bonds registration records of employees.

SEVEN YEARS

Accident reports and claims (settled cases), accounts payable and accounts receivable ledgers and schedules, canceled checks (But see under Permanent below), expired contracts and leases, expense analysis and distribution schedules, inventories of products, materials and supplies, invoices to customers, invoices from vendors, notes receivable ledgers and schedules, payroll records and summaries including payments to pensioners, plant cost ledgers, purchase orders (purchasing department copy), sales records, scrap and salvage records, canceled stock and bond certificates, subsidiary ledgers, time books, vouchers for payment to vendors, employees, etc. (includes allowances and reimbursement to employees, officers, etc. for travel and entertainment expenses.)

PERMANENTLY

Audit report of accountants, capital stock and bond records, ledgers transfer registrar, stubs showing issues, record of interest coupon, options, etc., cash books, charts of accounts, canceled checks for important payments, e.g. taxes, purchase of property, special contracts, etc., contracts and leases still in effect, correspondence (legal, and important matters only), deeds, mortgages, and bills of sale, depreciation schedules, financial statements (end of year), general and private ledgers , insurance records (current accident reports, claims, policies, etc.), journals, minute book of directors and stockholders including by-laws and charter, property appraisals by outside appraisers, property records, tax returns and worksheets, trade mark registrations.

ORDER FORM

You may order 'Bookkeeping and Administration for the Smaller Business' by completing the form below and mailing it to:

ETTA PUBLISHING
28605 LAKESHORE BLVD.
WILLOWICK, OHIO 44095

Please enclose your check or money order payable to the order of Etta Publishing.

Your book will be mailed within three business days.

NOTE: If you order five copies or more, please take a discount of 10% off the retail price.

■·
ORDER FORM

Please send me _____ copies of 'Bookkeeping and Administration for the Smaller Business' at $12.95 per copy:

Quantity_____times $12.95	$_____
Less 10% discount (5 or more copies)	_____
Shipping and handling ($2.39/copy)	_____
Total amount enclosed with order form	$_____
	================

Mail to: ETTA Publishing, 28605 Lakeshore Blvd., Willowick, Ohio 44095

ORDER FORM

You may order 'Bookkeeping and Administration for the Smaller Business' by completing the form below and mailing it to:

ETTA PUBLISHING
28605 LAKESHORE BLVD.
WILLOWICK, OHIO 44095

Please enclose your check or money order payable to the order of Etta Publishing.

Your book will be mailed within three business days.

NOTE: If you order five copies or more, please take a discount of 10% off the retail price.

■■

ORDER FORM

Please send me _____ copies of 'Bookkeeping and Administration for the Smaller Business' at $12.95 per copy:

Quantity_____times $12.95	$_____
Less 10% discount (5 or more copies)	_____
Shipping and handling ($2.39/copy)	_____
Total amount enclosed with order form	$_____
	================

Mail to: ETTA Publishing, 28605 Lakeshore Blvd., Willowick, Ohio 44095

ORDER FORM

You may order 'Bookkeeping and Administration for the Smaller Business' by completing the form below and mailing it to:

ETTA PUBLISHING
28605 LAKESHORE BLVD.
WILLOWICK, OHIO 44095

Please enclose your check or money order payable to the order of Etta Publishing.

Your book will be mailed within three business days.

NOTE: If you order five copies or more, please take a discount of 10% off the retail price.

- -

ORDER FORM

Please send me _____ copies of 'Bookkeeping and Administration for the Smaller Business' at $12.95 per copy:

Quantity_____times $12.95	$_____
Less 10% discount (5 or more copies)	_____
Shipping and handling ($2.39/copy)	_____
Total amount enclosed with order form	$_____
	================

Mail to: ETTA Publishing, 28605 Lakeshore Blvd., Willowick, Ohio 44095